Eastern Blocks

by
Zupagrafika

ZUPA
GRA
FiKA

Contents

The Iron Curtain was understood in the West as The Concrete Curtain. Everything behind it was perceived as mass produced and grey. People conveniently forgot that Chorweiler, Thamesmead, Chelmsley Wood and La Cité Rateau were on the 'right' side of the divide. Or perhaps they just assumed these examplars were the result of creeping Soviet influence. The truth is there is as much, if not more pure brutalism – cast in place concrete architecture that exhibits a ballsy visual flourish – in the West, plus a good deal of other modernism too. But the brutalism and the (shall we call it) 'marketplace modernism' - that is the cheaper, slightly shoddier deployment of concrete on a sublime scale, often utilising prefabricated panel systems and often for mass housing - when it appeared in the East, was always about spectacle. All post-War public life here, architecture included, was about 'the show'. If you thought PR was a slippery side-effect of capitalism, take a look at the supreme examples of promo films, photos, posters and books that tried to persuade everyone, their creators included, that everything in the communist world was ok. Highpoints of the spectacle include the Centre for Robotics, which brings the glamour of space and science to an arterial road in the Saint Petersburg suburbs.

Prefabricated panel block under
construction. Hungary, 1969
Fortepan Archives / Photo: Dr. Tóth Károly

Suburbs are where this book fixes its focus. Not the sometimes bucolic, always boring suburbs of semi detached houses on that sinking rock just North West of Calais where Sunday roasts are quite popular, but ballsy concoctions of many *rayons* and *microrayons* comprising serious buildings - Marzahn, Novosmolenskaya, Ursynów, Yasenevo and Újpalota. Sometimes the suburbs were so big they resembled new towns, like Halle-Neustadt (aka HaNeu) in South East Germany. HaNeu today is an example of gutsy grandeur meeting the realities of maintenance budgets – anguilliform walkways and *Plattenbau* blocks that aren't buffed or sheened look sad and crumbling. At least Poland, East Germany, Hungary and the USSR begat public housing and believed in it.

'The Iron Curtain was understood in the West as The Concrete Curtain. Everything behind it was perceived as mass produced and grey'

The walls could be thin, flats small, and developments monotonous; and Communism did not equal freedom, but cheap, public housing was one positive legacy of the Eastern Bloc, ditto public transport and public art – canorous social realist sculpture and gratifyingly bonkers public art adorn many developments, with their grand public spaces to play in. Meanwhile the showstoppers of the East are enjoying a second life today – Skopje and Novi Beograd will blow your mind, The House of The Aviators in Moscow (did Corbusier care about how many times he was ripped off?) and the

Plattenbausiedlung in the former GDR
SLUB Dresden / Deutsche Fotothek / Gerhard Weber

'UFO' protrusion of the Kiev State Scientific and Technical Library still fascinate. The future of these buildings is uncertain. Their ideology doesn't fit with the present and many are neglected or repainted in jaunty colours or privatised. Their enduring popularity among architects and critics says it all though.

Christopher Beanland

Author of *Concrete Concept* (Frances Lincoln, 2016)

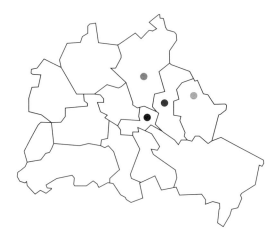

Friedrichshain	●	28
Lichtenberg	●	10, 13, 14, 15, 18, 19, 22, 23, 24
Marzahn	●	12, 16, 17, 20, 25, 26, 27, 29, 30, 31
Pankow	●	11, 21

(East) Berlin

It was in the 1950s when the first housing cooperative was established in Berlin's eastern district of Lichtenberg to provide homes for the employees of a local factory and their families. Two decades later, huge *Plattenbau* high-rises, snakes and slabs were mass-erected in Fennpfuhl, Friedrichsfelde and other parts of the area. From the simple WBS 70 prefabricated panel system to its more sophisticated versions, like the WHH-GT 84/85 *Hochhaus* special, more and more districts followed suit and constructed similar concrete collective accommodation units. Central heating, private bathrooms, lifts and communal greenery became symbols of modern socialist living, which lured thousands of East Berliners to settle in Marzahn – one of the largest mass housing estates in Berlin. At the same time, on the other side of the Wall, Walter Gropius started to shape his dashing urban plan of Gropiusstadt for Neukölln, taking prefab panel construction to the next level. Over recent decades, however, Berlin's post-war modernist estates have earned a rather bad reputation and their future is uncertain; some are up for extensive renovations, while others await proximate demolition.

Frankfurter Allee *Hochhaus* entrances | *Plattenbau* WHH-GT 18/21

Built: 1970s | Lichtenberg

Ernst-Thälmann-Park *Hochhäuser*. Lilli-Henoch-Straße | *Plattenbau* WHH - GT 84/85 ETP
Built: mid-1980s | Prenzlauer Berg, Pankow

Erstmal zu Penny.
Herzlich Willkommen!
Montag – Samstag
07:00 – 21:00
PENNY.

Recently renovated *Plattenbau Hochhaus* in Scheibenbergstraße | Marzahn

Regenbogenhaus. Möllendorffstraße | Built: late 1970s | Fennpfuhl, Lichtenberg

◁◁

Haus 15, headquarters of the former
Ministry for State Security (Stasi).
Ruschestraße | Built: 1970s
Lichtenberg

△

Tierhof Marzahn
Landsberger Allee
Marzahn

Helene-Weigel-Platz *Doppelhochhäuser Typ* SK 65 | Built: mid-1980s | Marzahn

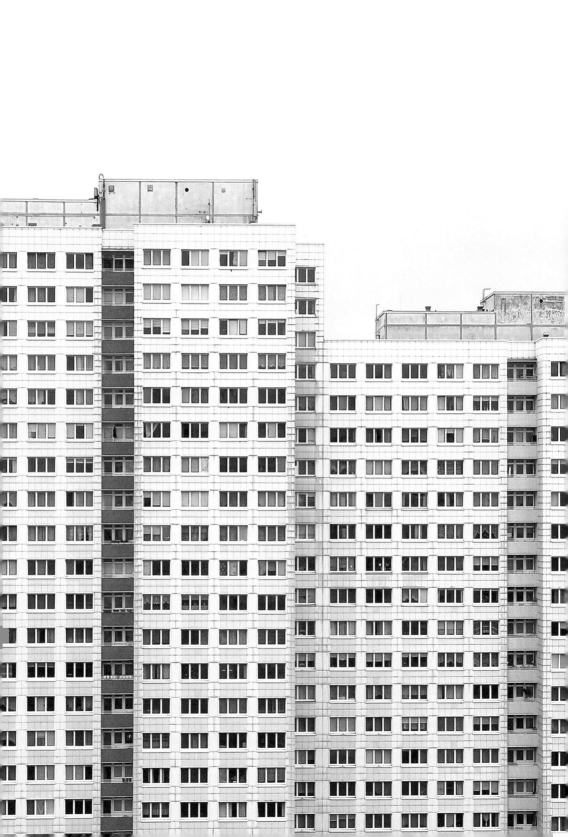

◁◁

Frankfurter Allee
Plattenbau WHH-GT 18/21
Built: 1970s | Lichtenberg

△

Kino Sojus. Helene-Weigel-Platz
Operating from 1981 to 2007
Marzahn

Ella-Kay-Straße | *Plattenbau* WBS 70 | Built: 1980s | Prenzlauer Berg, Pankow

Tiled *Plattenbausiedlung*. Rosenfelder Ring | Friedrichsfelde, Lichtenberg

Herzbergstraße *Hochhaus* | Built: 1970s | Fennpfuhl, Lichtenberg

Zingster Straße *Hochhäuser* | *Plattenbau* WHH - GT 84/85 | Built: mid-1980s. Renovated: 1997

24   Neu-Hohenschönhausen, Lichtenberg

Marzahner Promenade *Hochhäuser* | *Plattenbau* WHH - GT 84/85 | Built: 1980s | Marzahn

◁◁
Housing complex in Märkische Allee
Built: 1970s
Marzahn

△
Straße der Pariser Kommune
Plattenbau WBS 70 | Built: 1980s
Friedrichshain

Ludwig-Renn-Straße | Built: 1970s | Marzahn

Allee der Kosmonauten
Plattenbau from the 1970s
Marzahn

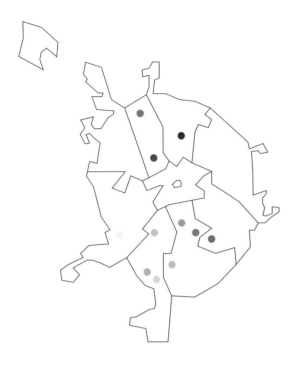

Moscow

The industrial housing experiment revolutionized urbanization during the Soviet era. Thousands of new dwellings could now be erected quicker and cheaper than ever before. The first prefab panel slabs built in the Moscow district of Cheryomushki were widely 'copied and pasted' into dozens of new micro-districts springing up around the Russian capital between the 1960s and 1980s. Their clones would take different forms and colours, giving each microrayon a tiny bit of their own unique identity. Two circular *Bublik* houses built for the 1980 Summer Olympics remain landmarks of Ochakovo-Matveyevskoye, while blue and red facades of *peshka* blocks towering above the South-Western Administrative Okrug will guide your way to Konkovo or Yasenevo. Today, the 'sleeping districts' are homes to the vast majority of Muscovites and the monumental cityscapes they form are beyond striking. However, it is not only the peripheries that exhibit a modernist approach to post-war housing architecture in Moscow. Walking around the areas of Danilovsky or Alexeyevsky, you will stumble upon a good number of captivating designs, such as the pilotis-supported 'House on Chicken Legs' or the mighty 'Titanic'.

◁◁

Residential complex in ul. Severnoye
Chertanovo | Built: 1970s
Chertanovo Severnoye District

△ | ▷

'The House on Chicken Legs'
Prospekt Mira | Built: 1968
Alexeyevsky District

Hotel Kosmos. Prospekt Mira | Built: 1979 | Alexeyevsky District

'The Titanic' residential building. Ul. Bolshaya Tulskaya | Built: 1986 | Danilovsky District

Ul. Ostrovityanova | Built: mid-1980s | Konkovo District

'Brezhnevka' in ul. Generala Dorokhova | Built: mid-1980s | Ochakovo-Matveyevskoye District

　　Nagatinskaya Embankment　|　Built: mid-1980s　|　Nagatinsky Zaton District

△

Prefabricated panel from the 1970s
Ochakovo-Matveyevskoye District

▷▷

Novoyasenevskiy Prospekt housing complex
Built: mid-1980s | Yasenevo District

P-44 panel block in ul. Akademika Pilyugina | Built: mid-1980s | Lomonosovsky District

Ul. Yasnogorskaya | Built: mid-1980s | Yasenevo District

Precast high-rise tower blocks in ul. Guryanova | Built: 1990s | Pechatniki District

Peshka block in ul. Krasnopolyanskaya with the *rayon* name written on top | Built: mid-1980s | Zapadnoye Degunino District   49

'Bublik' residential complex
Ul. Nezhinskaya | Built: 1972
Ochakovo-Matveyevskoye District

△ | ▷

'The Centipede' or 'The House of the Aviators'
Ul. Begovaya | Built: 1978
Begovoy District

Tiled *peshka* in ul. Ostrovityanova
Built: mid-1980s
Konkovo District

Lenin Komsomol Automobile Plant Museum
Ul. Shosseynaya
Built: 1975-1980 | Pechatniki District

Białołęka	●	68
Bielany	●	64, 62, 66, 67
Mokotów	●	72, 73, 76, 77
Praga Północ	●	74
Śródmieście	●	61, 63, 65, 69
Targówek	●	60, 75
Ursynów	●	70, 71

Warsaw

Thousands of concrete prefab panels were mass-produced by 'house factories' scattered around Warsaw suburbia in the 1970s. The innovative construction system marked the beginning of a new era in urban planning and started a real housing boom in post-war Poland. Huge cranes on the vast, empty suburban areas of Białołęka or Ursynów became postcards from the 'golden epoque' of The Polish People's Republic. The panels were assembled in rows of functionalist blocks following fixed patterns, adjusted to the necessities of each district. Despite notorious technical issues and strict housing norms in terms of square meters per family, *wielka płyta* proved to be a cure for the housing shortage and poor living conditions – much appreciated by those who were lucky enough to be granted their own flats; 'cramped but mine' is a popular Polish saying, rooted in the *PRL* times. Today, houses made in factories coexist with 'the concrete monoliths' that can be found in the centre of the Polish capital. When visiting the former Warsaw Jewish Ghetto, you may be surprised to find yourself in the middle of Za Żelazną Bramą, a large-scale estate erected on its remains and shaping one of the most unique landmarks of the city.

Targówek Mieszkaniowy Estate. Ul. Trocka | Built: late 1970s | Targówek

Za Żelazną Bramą Estate. Ul. Marszałkowska | Built: 1965-1972 | Śródmieście Północne

Tower blocks in ul. Klaudyny | Built: 1970s
Marymont-Ruda, Bielany

The Hammer' high-rise. Ul. Smolna 8 | Built: 1976 | Śródmieście Północne

Renovated tower blocks in ul. Kwitnąca | Built: late 1970s | Chomiczówka, Bielany

Torwar Estate. Ul. Fabryczna | Built: 1971-1973 | Solec, Śródmieście

Residential building in
ul. Gwiaździsta | Built: 1970s
Marymont-Ruda, Bielany

Wielka płyta blocks in ul. Van Gogha | Built: late 1970s | Tarchomin, Białołęka

Torwar Estate. Ul. Fabryczna | Built: 1971-1973 | Solec, Śródmieście

◁◁

Wielka płyta block in ul. Janowskiego
Built: late 1970s | Jary, Ursynów

△

H-shaped tower block. Ul. Modzelewskiego
Built: 1970s | Służew, Mokotów

'Club 100', property of the Russian embassy. Ul. Sobieskiego | Built: 1977-1978. Currently abandoned | Sielce, Mokotów

'Kolonia Białostocka' Estate. Al. Solidarności | Built: mid-1980s | Szmulowizna, Praga Północ

Toruńska Estate. Ul. Toruńska | Built: 1970s | Bródno, Targówek

△ | ▷

Start Hotel Aramis. Ul. Mangalia | Built: 1970s | Stegny, Mokotów

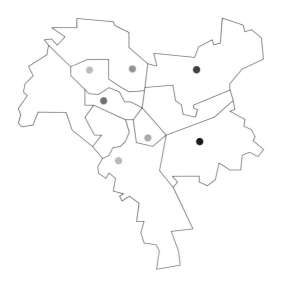

Darnytskyi	●	83, 94, 95
Desnianskyi	●	80, 93
Holosiivskyi	●	84, 85, 91, 96, 98, 99
Obolonskyi	●	88, 89, 90
Pecherskyi	●	81, 82
Podilskyi	●	87, 92, 97
Shevchenkivskyi	●	86

Kyiv

Colourful mosaics, rectangular tiles and geometrical facade decor resembling Ukrainian folk motifs were commonly applied to raw concrete, which, after WW2, was used to rebuild the capital of the Ukrainian Soviet Socialist Republic. These distinctive elements made Kyiv's post-war modernist architecture stand out among other identical units mass-built all around the former USSR and, to this day, define the landscapes of Vynohradar and Teremky estates. These and other housing developments made of prefabricated panels (manufactured in *ZBK* factories) are commonly referred to as 'panelky' and seem to have proved so efficient in Soviet times that new districts, such as Pozniaky, are still being constructed out of concrete prefab elements today. Modernist ideas gaining ground in post-war Ukraine materialized not only as functionalist residential estates to house the rapidly growing population in the 1960s and 1970s, but also took the more sophisticated shapes of the State Scientific and Technical Library or the streamlined Crematorium, leading Kyiv towards a new, modern future.

Tiled facades in vul. Kashtanova
Built: 1980s | Troieshchyna,
Desnianskyi District

▷

'The Flying Saucer' State Scientific
and Technical Library. Vul. Antonovycha
Built: 1971 | Pecherskyi District

Pecherskyi Universam, aka 'Baraban'. Vul. Panasa Myrnoho | Built: 1984 | Pecherskyi District

Post-Soviet *panelky* slab in vul. Anny Akhmatovoi | Pozniaky, Darnytskyi District

◁◁

Crematorium 'Halls of Farewell'.
Memory Park, Baikova Hill
Built: 1968-1981 | Holosiivskyi District

△

Soviet mosaic in Prospekt Peremohy
Built: late 1960s
Shuliavka, Shevchenkivskyi District

Tiled *panelky* in Prospekt Vasylya Poryka | Built: 1970s | Vynohradar, Podilskyi District

Residential tower blocks in Obolonskyi Prospekt | Built: 1981 | Obolon, Obolonskyi District

Large panel system residential building in Obolonskyi Prospekt | Built: 1970s | Obolon, Obolonskyi District

The Faculty of Physics. T. Shevchenko University. Vul. Sofii Kovalevskoi | Built: 1972-1980 | Holosiivskyi District

Residential block in Prospekt Heorhiya Honhadze | Built: 1980s | Vynohradar, Podilskyi District

△

▷▷

Playground in vul. Honoré de Balzac
Troieshchyna, Desnianskyi District

Sonyachne Lake. Vul. Revutskoho
Pozniaky, Darnytskyi District

△

T. Shevchenko University
Vul. Sofii Kovalevskoi | Built: 1972-1980
Holosiivskyi District

▷▷

Teremky Estate. Prospekt Akademika Hlushkova
Built: 1980s | Holosiivskyi District
(p. 98-99)

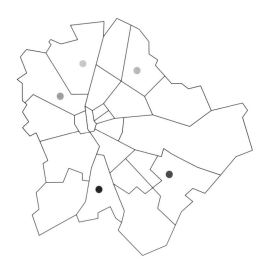

Csepel	●	102, 103
Havanna	●	109, 110, 112, 113
Óbuda	●	107
Országút	●	106
Újpalota	●	104, 105, 108, 111

Budapest

Endless rows of *panelház* were all you could see on the horizon of the Budapest hinterlands in the 1970s. In response to rapid growth of the city's population after WW2, the communist government drafted a five-year economic plan for Hungary, which involved new housing for everyone. As with the experimental district of Óbuda – a seminal prefabricated panel micro-city built in the 1960s – 'house factories' quickly sprang up in other suburbs, giving rise to new concrete 'colonies' made of two types of prefabricated units – the Lars-Nielsen, originating in Denmark and commonly used to rebuild western European cities, and the Soviet large panel system type. Due to its functionality and affordability, the latter has monopolized the outskirts of Budapest for decades. The new *lakótelepek* (housing estates) were an assortment of different shapes, which could be assembled out of precast panels. High-rises, slabs and concrete zigzags were copied from building type catalogues, and pasted onto the urban landscape of Havanna, Újpalota or Csepel. Given their limited life span and increasingly troublesome maintenance, new solutions are being sought to the problems of renovation and preservation of these buildings, which have been home to thousands of Budapestians over the years.

◁◁

Csepel water tower
Kossuth Lajos utca | Built: 1984
Csepel-Erdőalja, District XXI

△ | ▷

'Víztoronyhàz' residential building and water tower
Nyírpalota út | Built: 1973-1975
Újpalota, District XV

Hotel Budapest. Szilágyi Erzsébet fasor | Built: 1967 | Országút, District II

Ágoston utca | Built: late 1980s | Óbuda, District III

Nyírpalota út | Built: 1970s | Újpalota, District XV

Panelház in Havanna utca | Built: late 1970s | Havanna, District XVIII

△

Prefabricated panel blocks
in Nyírpalota út | Built: 1970s
Újpalota, District XV

▷▷

Barta Lajos utca
Built: late 1970s
Havanna, District XVIII

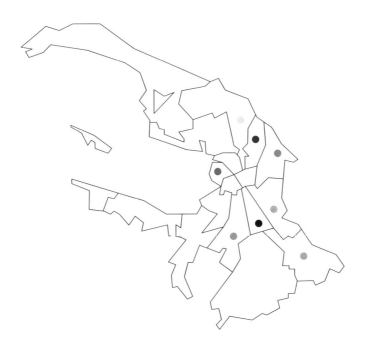

Frunzensky	●	124
Kalininsky	●	127, 133, 134, 135
Kolpinsky	●	128, 136, 139
Krasnogvardeysky	●	125
Moskovsky	●	121, 126, 129
Nevsky	●	122, 123
Vasileostrovsky	●	116, 117, 118, 119, 132, 137, 138
Vyborgsky	●	120, 130, 131, 140, 141

Saint Petersburg

In the face of the post-war housing crisis in Russia, the famous *kommunalki* were still homes to many urbanites of Saint Petersburg. Since the 19th century, these communal flats have been used to accommodate multiple families from all walks of life and social backgrounds under one roof in the spirit of collective living. In the mid-1950s, when Khrushchev became the First Secretary of the Communist Party, city dwellers were granted more space and privacy, as the government started mass construction of five-storey housing units made of brick or concrete panels. These earned the nickname *khrushchyovki*. The new approach to collective housing would then be implemented on a larger scale outside city centres in the form of concrete high-rises quickly assembled out of prefabricated elements. *Brezhnevki* erected between the 1960s and 1970s, named after the new USSR leader Leonid Brezhnev, together with large panel system blocks and monolithic reinforced concrete constructions, shaped the panorama of Saint Petersburg's suburban developments. The new neighbourhoods springing around the peripheral microrayons today seem like chips off the old Soviet blocks, only their scale gets bigger and bigger.

Reinforced concrete housing complex. Novosmolenskaya Embankment | Built: 1986 | Vasileostrovsky District

'Vasileostrovet' Garage Cooperative. Ul. Uralskaya | Built: 1985 | Vasileostrovsky District

Tiled *panelki* block in Severnyy Prospekt | Built: mid-1970s | Vyborgsky District

'Dom-Plastina' high-rise tower block. Moskovsky Prospekt | Built: 1973-1975 | Moskovsky District

◁◁

Residential complex on the Oktyabrskaya
Embankment | Built: early 1970s | Nevsky District

△

New skyline of the
Frunzensky District

New residential estate in the Krasnogvardeysky District | Built: 2015

Twin residential tower blocks in Ploshchad Pobedy | Built: 1973-1975 | Moskovsky District

Electromera Scientific Research Institute. Prospekt Prosvescheniya | Built: early 1980s | Kalininsky District

Prefabricated panel blocks by the Izhora River. Bulvar Trudyaschikhsya
Built: early 1980s | Kolpinsky District

Dormitory of the Saint Petersburg Law Institute. Ul. Kostyushko | Built: 1980 | Moskovsky District

'Brezhnevka' in busy Prospekt
Prosveshcheniya | Built: 1980s
Vyborgsky District

△
Brick housing unit. Ul. Beringa
Built: early 1970s
Vasileostrovsky District

'The Shamrocks' tower blocks in Severnyy Prospekt | Built: 1975-1980 | Kalininsky District

Russian State Scientific Center
for Robotics and Technical
Cybernetics. Tikhoretskiy Prospekt
Built: 1973-1986 | Kalininsky District

Ul. Proletarskaya | Built: 1970s | Kolpinsky District

Residential building on the Morskaya Embankment | Built: 1980s | Vasileostrovsky District

△

Ul. Korablestroiteley
Built: 1979
Vasileostrovsky District

▷

Prefabricated panel block
Ul. Izhorskogo Batalona
Built: 1980s | Kolpinsky District

▷▷

Panelki block in ul.
Khoshimina | Built: 1989
Vyborgsky District

Index of Architects

Author

Zupagrafika are David Navarro and Martyna Sobecka, an independent publisher, author and graphic design studio, established in 2012 in Poznań, Poland, celebrating modernist architecture, design and photography in a unique and playful way.

For almost a decade, David and Martyna have been documenting brutalist landmarks and different types of precast panel constructions scattered around European suburbia. The photography archive built up in the course of this research has provided a significant frame of reference for their architectural paper models and books. *Eastern Blocks* showcases snapshots from Zupagrafika's winter journeys around central and eastern Europe, accompanied by a selection of images specially taken for this book by local photographers.

Since 2012, Zupagrafika has designed, illustrated and published architectural kits and books showcasing post-war concrete constructions in Poland, such as *Miasto Blok-How* (2012), *Blok Wschodni* (2014) and *Blokowice* (2016). In 2015, they created the 'Brutal London' series, documenting brutalist architecture in London at risk of disappearing. The collection quickly attracted worldwide attention and was translated into the book *Brutal London: Construct Your Own Concrete Capital* (Prestel, 2016). Zupagrafika's subsequent publications include *Brutal East* (2017), *The Constructivist* (2017), *Modern East* (2017), *Brutal Britain* (2018), *Hidden Cities* (2018), *Panelki* (2019), *Eastern Blocks* (2019), *Concrete Siberia* (2020), *Brutal Poland* (2020), and *Monotowns* (2021).

Acknowledgements

Zupagrafika would like to thank Alexander Veryovkin, Tatiana Kabakova, Christopher Beanland, Balázs Csizik, Vadym Bilyk, Anastasiia Oksiukovska, Maciej Kabsch, Marta & Maciej Mach, Maciej Frąckowiak, Paquita & Pepe, Kasia & Paweł, Andrés Navarro, Judit, Rita & Simón for their help and support; as well as Fortepan and Deutsche Fotothek archives.

Contributors

David Navarro & Martyna Sobecka (Zupagrafika): see Author p. 143 (photos of Berlin, Kyiv and Warsaw).

Alexander Veryovkin: photographer born in Leningrad, USSR; based in Saint Petersburg, Russia (commissioned photos of Moscow and Saint Petersburg).

Balázs Csizik: visual artist and lecturer based in Budapest, Hungary (commissioned photos of Budapest).

Christopher Beanland (foreword): novelist and journalist who writes about architecture and cities. He has contributed to *The Independent*, *The Guardian*, *The Telegraph* and *BBC*, among other newspapers and magazines. He is the author of *Concrete Concept* (Frances Lincoln, 2016) and the novel *The Wall In The Head* (Unbound, 2019).

—

Published by Zupagrafika
Poznań, Poland. 2019

Printed in Poland
Paper from responsible sources
ISBN 978-83-950574-3-4
www.zupagrafika.com